Created by Wild Pages Press 2017

Made in the USA
Monee, IL
15 July 2021

73699370R00085